# little dreams

Nancy A. Moore

*Printed in the United States of America*

ISBN: 978-0-9851721-7-6

Nancy A. Moore © 2012
Digitally Reproduced by
Converpage Digital Reproductions
23 Acorn Street
Scituate, MA 02066
www.converpage.com

To freedom –
Much love always

# A Shark Story

I have experienced domestic violence. I don't like to think of myself as a victim, but I'm proud to be a survivor because it took a lot of courage. I struggled to understand how this happened to me, because I thought I was too smart, too normal or too experienced in life to have this happen.

It was as if I grew up in a place where ever since I was young the natural practically inevitable thing was to grow up and swim with a dolphin happily ever after. So as I grew up I met a few dolphins and even swam with some for a while, but none of these were the dolphin for me to swim with happily ever after.

On the other side of the island, there was a shark watching the dolphins swim, and he wanted to swim happily ever after too. He tried it a few times, but when women saw the shark, they refused to go out and swim with him. So he learned to act like a dolphin. Sometimes he got someone to swim with him for a while, but it wouldn't last.

A long time went by and I hadn't swum with anybody. And then I saw what I thought was a dolphin swim by, beckoning me to come with him. I could hardly believe my good luck! I jumped in and swam around for a while, enjoying what it felt like to swim with a dolphin again.

But then one day I noticed a tooth that looked like a shark's tooth in the dolphin's mouth. I thought maybe I just imagined it, but after I saw a few more teeth, I knew they were real. Some of the teeth looked like this: getting out of proportion emotionally during a disagreement, refusing to leave my house when asked, jealousy, not wanting me to talk to my friends on the phone, and competing with my son for my attention.

I began to realize I was swimming with a shark. I must have looked nervous because the shark said to me, "Don't worry, I know I have these sharp teeth, but I would never use them to hurt you." But despite his best efforts, when he got angry with me, he bit me. Some of his bites consisted of: lying to me, verbally abusing me, accusations that I was unfaithful, grabbing the steering wheel of the car while I was driving, and physically pushing me around.

I said I didn't want to swim with him anymore, but he told me how lonely he was before I came along and pleaded with me to stay. He said, "I want the life of a dolphin, and I will do whatever it takes to swim with you. Even go to counseling or go on medication. I promise I'll change."

So we went to counseling, but still he sometimes acted like a shark. He went on medication, but still he sometimes acted like a shark. Although there were times he made progress, and although he was always sorry, sometimes he bit me and it really hurt. Some of these bites looked like this: refusing to leave my house during fights, causing me to have to leave my own home to get away from him, preventing me from leaving the house during fights so I couldn't get away from him, threatening to let my dogs out into the street to be hit by a car if I left the house, physically pinning me down and not letting me up, kicking down the front door when I locked him out of my house, threatening to beat people up that he thought I liked, threatening to cause a scene and hurt people at my son's 8th grade graduation, kicking my car and putting a dent in it, and ripping up paperwork that I had spent months putting together.

During all this time, I began acting less like myself. I used to be a happy swimmer, splashing about, enjoying the water and rarely getting upset. But when the shark would start to come after me, I would scream and yell at him to get away. I was turning into someone who screamed and yelled so much, sometimes I almost lost my voice. I didn't like who I was becoming, and I didn't like my life.

I realized that if I stayed with the shark I was going to keep getting hurt, maybe even much worse. But I also realized that although the shark felt bad about my injuries, he liked having someone to swim with, and he would not willingly let me go.

I thought once the shark knew I was leaving he would get so mad he would bite me worse than he ever had before, even if that meant he would be hunted down and punished later for doing it. But I couldn't stand swimming with the shark anymore, and sometimes I started feeling like I didn't even want to try to keep swimming at all and it might be better if I drowned.

I didn't think I could make it back to shore before he caught up with me if I tried to swim for it. But one day after a particularly nasty bite I knew I had to try. So I swam for it and he chased me. Some of his chasing looked like this: calling me constantly so that the only way to get any peace was to turn the phone off (eliminating my ability to communicate with anyone else) until I could get my telephone numbers changed, threatening me, and threatening to throw a rock through the window and beat the first person out the door with a baseball bat if I invited my family over for Christmas.

I debated whether to try to get a restraining order against him. I researched them online and went to the courthouse to ask about them, but it seemed like the only reason to get one was if I was in fear of my life, and I wasn't sure my situation was that bad. I think if I admitted to myself my situation was that bad, I would have been too terrified to function.

But when things didn't improve, I went to the police station and spoke with one of the officers about whether to get one or not. She told me what I already suspected - sometimes it works out, and sometimes getting one makes things worse.

Finally, he threatened to go after my son, since he said I didn't seem to be afraid enough of him anymore. Then I was terrified and I knew I had to try for the restraining order. I went to court the next morning and got a temporary restraining order good for a couple of days until they could have a hearing so he could tell his side of the story. After receiving the temporary order he tried to discredit me with the police saying I was calling him. In court he denied the threats he'd made. But I still had many of the threatening voice mail messages saved and offered to let the judge listen to them. The judge didn't even need to listen. I was granted a restraining order for a year, telling him to stay away from me and my son, and not to contact us.

But shortly after, he began to call me at work. The first time he called he asked me not to report it and said he wouldn't call again. And I didn't, hoping that was true. I didn't even know what police station to call to report the violation, or if I had to go to the police station, or how long it would take. But it was a mistake not to report it right away because he kept calling and after a few calls I did report it, but the first thing the policeman asked me was why I hadn't reported it right away.

He was arrested, but he still kept on coming. This looked like: somehow getting my new cell phone number and having his son call me, calling my ex-husband, mailing me an unsigned note, and sending me text messages.

I reported all the violations and eventually he was arrested a second time. A year after the initial restraining order was given, I had a chance to either let it expire or go to court and ask for an extension. My counselor encouraged me to request a permanent extension and I did. Upon notification, he violated the order by calling me on my cell phone to tell me he didn't expect me to make it permanent.

After getting some distance away from the relationship, and with the help of counseling and a group or two, here's what I have learned:

1. Any woman could mistake a shark for a dolphin when the shark is disguised as a dolphin.

2. All kinds of women can look good to a shark regardless of age, appearance or education.

3. Sharks are unable to keep the promises they make because their shark nature is stronger.

4. Sharks don't turn into dolphins.

5. If a shark has to choose between being alone and making my life better, or having company and making my life worse, the shark will choose company.

Some good things have come from this experience:

1. I am now a much stronger swimmer.

2. I don't mind swimming alone as much as I once did.

3. Now I am much more apt to recognize a shark very quickly and swim away immediately if I meet up with one.

4. When I have to choose between a better life or a worse life for me, I chose a better life.

5. Surviving such a dangerous situation prompted me to fulfill a lifelong dream of traveling to France that I had been too afraid to pursue before. The things I was afraid of – plane crashes, terrorists, not speaking the language – didn't seem so bad to me after being afraid in my own home. So I flew to France by myself, met up with a tour group and had the vacation of a lifetime.

I didn't figure out that I was swimming with a shark until we were already getting far from the shore. If I had known the little things that happened in the beginning would inevitably get worse, maybe I could have made a break for shore while I was still close.

But I waited, at first hoping things would get better and we could stay together. Then I waited hoping it would enable me to get away safely.

I'm very grateful that my situation has calmed down considerably. Looking back on things I believed there was supposed to be a dolphin in my life so I was predisposed to see a dolphin. I expected so much to have a dolphin to swim with I forgot that life has more to offer me than dolphins or sharks. I wanted it so much I forgot to notice that if my life wasn't better swimming with someone else, then why would I want to?

I hope telling my story will help others to recognize if they might also be swimming with a shark, to know that it only gets worse, and to swim for shore at the opportune moment.

## Passing Time

The restraining order in my pocketbook hasn't been taken out or opened in a couple of years now. I still keep it with me at all times in case the situation ever arises where I need it, but I'm hoping that it will remain untouched.

While I was hip deep in the relationship that ultimately led to that little piece of legal paper in my purse, I could only see bits and snatches of what was happening. I could only tell people little pieces of the story. For a long time I was in the in between place, knowing I needed to get out of that relationship, but also knowing it was going to be a scary, tricky piece of work to get away.

Now that some time has passed, I have compassion for myself where I used to have blame. The experience has changed me deeply but maybe for the better. In hindsight, it's not the road I would have chosen to make improvements, but at the time it must have seemed like the way to go, or I wouldn't have gone there.

I feel pretty good lately. It took a long time to get here. But now I realize I was in the worst kind of war. My enemy was disguised as my friend. The battle took place in my home. For a long time I didn't feel safe but I couldn't show it for fear the enemy would go from small attacks here and there to a full blown assault. I couldn't admit the truth to myself about what was happening, so I split myself in two between what I wanted to believe and what was really going on.

I survived. Like in Bonnie Raitt's song, I bent pretty low, but I didn't break.

## Unfulfilled Desires

I believe in a higher power with my whole heart (or maybe it's just with part of my heart, since I do question a lot, and wonder what's going on with certain things), although I didn't for a long time. I believe in a higher power that's good and personally involved in my life to the extent I allow it. I don't mind using the word God as the name for my higher power, so I do. God has done so many wonderful things for me including keeping me sober. I'm not complaining and I do appreciate all the miracles that have come to me. It's just that I've wanted to be part of a couple for a long time and it's mainly been an unfulfilled desire.

There's a passage in Melody Beattie's <u>The Language of Letting Go</u> daily reading book for March 29th that says,

"Picture yourself walking through a meadow. There is a path opening before you. As you walk, you feel hungry. Look to your left. There's a fruit tree in full bloom. Pick what you need.

Steps later, you notice you're thirsty. On your right, there's a fresh water spring.

When you are tired, a resting place emerges. When you are lonely, a friend appears to walk with you. When you get lost, a teacher with a map appears.

Before long, you notice the flow: need and supply, desire and fulfillment. Maybe, you wonder, Someone gave me the need because Someone planned to fulfill it. Maybe I had to feel the need, so I would notice and accept the gift. Maybe closing my eyes to the desire closes my arms to its fulfillment.

Demand and supply, desire and fulfillment – a continuous cycle, unless we break it. All the necessary supplies have already been planned and provided for this journey.

Today, everything I need shall be supplied to me."

It's my favorite passage in the whole book, and when I read it I felt like it was too good to be true, but I really, really wanted it to be true. I thought it meant that God would give me a guy to be with because I was feeling pretty thirsty for one. Now that I reread the passage though, I see it mentions providing food, water and rest, but no actual men or sex. I may have overreached the bounds of the message in my original interpretation.

My sister says maybe I'm not in a relationship because I'm supposed to be writing this and if I were with someone, I wouldn't have the time or the inclination. She could be right. But my heart still hurts sometimes on this subject.

Tracy Chapman asks in her song, "If everything you think you know, makes your life unbearable, would you change?" I would like to, and I think I am slowly changing. It's tough, because what I think I know seems like it must be true, but I'm learning to question my beliefs, especially the one that says it's important to be in a "relationship."

I used to be so consumed by the desire to be in a relationship with a guy that I was almost always in one. Then I went through a phase where I would have long periods of being single interspersed with sporadic failed attempts at relationships. But I think they failed because I was getting healthier.

Despite my sideways notice that the parts of my life when I was single seemed to be happier than when I was with someone, it didn't alter my consuming desire to find the right partner. I thought if I made sufficient spiritual progress, God would provide me with that right partner. Since I had been working on spiritual progress for a while, I was pretty surprised when the next relationship I was in turned out to be the most difficult, least suitable for me so far. I was expecting wonderful so much that it took me a while to notice I was getting farther away from happiness, not closer to it.

Being with Dick had many unexpected explosions, like I imagine there would be in a war zone. All the issues in my previous relationships combined couldn't hold a candle to the difficulty of that last relationship. Now most of the time I enjoy being single in a way I never could before, because I have that war zone to compare it to. These days I much prefer peace, and I'm still grateful for it every day.

Mostly I would have to say God is doing a pretty good job, although I didn't expect my last relationship to be my worst yet. I thought that as I made spiritual progress my life would become easier and more peaceful. I thought since I was trying to practice spiritual principles, the light shining in me would bring out the best in the other person. Even if things didn't work out I thought it would be easy for us to let go.

But I think a big change was required in me for me to be able to be in a healthy relationship with a man. I would focus on the guy and lose myself. I wanted it too much, so I was willing to give up far too much in the hopes of getting or keeping the relationship. Maybe for such a big change to take place within me, the enormous challenge of Dick was required.

I read an article in Oprah magazine (February 2008 issue) by Martha Beck that talked about when making a list of what you want works and when it doesn't. She described the shallows as a place where people are coming from fear when they make their list. I think I was always coming from a place of fear and desperate need when I wanted a guy in my life to somehow make me feel better. She talked about the inner core of peace, and coming from this place, making a list works. In this place, the person doesn't feel like they need the thing they want. They know they are OK without it. To get from the shallows to the inner core of peace a person has to go through the ring of fire. I think my relationship with Dick was my ring of fire.

Before Dick, as much as I wanted not to want a relationship too much, I knew I still did. After Dick, I still feel like it would be nice with the right person but I am not feeling desperate about it inside me. Maybe the only thing that could have gotten me off that one track theme of wanting to be in a relationship was something as difficult and awful as what I went through.

Change is so hard for me. Just wanting it has not been enough for me to make it happen. I want to be so loose and flexible that I'm like a leaf on a stream and I can be guided with a feather to veer right or left. But I'm really like a rusty old nut, stuck tightly on the rusty bolt of my old ideas and beliefs. It takes an incredibly strong, sometime repetitive yank with a big wrench, to get me loose. My spiritual practices were probably like a little "Nuts Off" lubricant for rusty bolts – just enough to enable the nut to be turned at all with the utmost force by the wrench, not nearly enough to be able to easily unscrew it by hand.

So the nut has turned a little bit - I have changed some. Also, I was able to finally do something I always wanted to do but never had the courage. I finally went on a trip to Southern France to fulfill a little dream. To get the courage to do that I went through this difficult, abusive relationship and found a way to come out the other side, with the help of God's wrench.

## Hearts and Smarts

Recently one of my co-workers asked me if I heard about the latest sensational murder. I asked what happened, and she said a woman doctor shot her husband after he had apparently beaten and abused her for years. My co-worker commented, "I don't understand how someone smart enough to become a doctor stayed in a situation like that all this time."

But I think I do. First of all, hearts aren't commanded by brains, and although hearts might not think very well, they feel much louder than a head can think. Secondly, there's a certain lack of imagination or lack of horrible experiences in someone who can't think of how a person could stay. How about threatening to kill her children if she told and/or left him? A man recently killed himself and his two children to get back at a wife or girlfriend who tried to get away by lighting them all on fire inside his car. What about if he threatened to kill her mother? I saw a girl on TV with half a face, who was shot and almost killed by her boyfriend. The boyfriend did kill her mother in the same incident. How about blackmail… maybe he knew something she did wrong – drinking, taking an illegal drug - and threatened to have her license to practice medicine revoked. Then there's the sheer desire to avoid the pain of having people know what's happening in your life, just how shitty it really is, feeling it's your own fault. Knowing that no restraining order can really protect you from someone hell bent on hurting you. Maybe the first time it happened when she was strongest and it was her best chance to leave it took her by such surprise that she was too stunned to do anything. And then, once she didn't do anything the first time, feeling how could she explain that the second time, or the third, or the fiftieth? After a while maybe the life force in her was beaten down so badly that even when the cage door was left open she didn't think to try and get out anymore. Maybe she didn't feel like she could outrun anybody anymore after all those physical and/or emotional beatings. And maybe knowing the guy well enough to know how dangerous he might be, and at the same time knowing him well enough to have seen the human side of him that no one else sees, she recognized the person inside the monster and didn't want to hurt that already so hurt person in trying to save herself. Until finally she realized and accepted that she had to hurt him to save herself.

When I looked back in my journal's entries during the time after I first met my ex-boyfriend Dick, I said I fell in love with him. At the time I wrote that I thought of it as a good thing.  But now I think, if I was dancing all along the edge of a cliff, out where a strong wind could blow me off balance and I could easily topple over the edge, then did I fall in love with him, or did I just fall?

## My Life is not a Movie

I wanted to be in a relationship too much. It's been true of me for most of my life, at least since my first divorce. The saying "You've got to love yourself first, before you can love someone else" struck terror in my heart because I knew somewhere inside that I was looking for the love I didn't have for myself through someone else. If that was doomed to failure, I was in trouble.

My Mom said to me once, "You think your life is a movie," meaning I needed to stop thinking my life was going to end like a romantic comedy. Maybe she was right. I watch, practically memorize, some movies where romance triumphs in the most unlikely circumstances to people who deserve to be happy. I'd like to be one of them.

Lately I've been thinking it would be better for me if I didn't watch my collection of romantic comedies for a while. It's probably true that this kind of dream can and does come true or there wouldn't be so many stories about it. But it may also be true that romantic love is only one dream that can come true in a person's life and lots of other dreams could feel good and make them happy. Maybe the romantic dream is like a big advertisement by the romantic comedy movie makers, and the Valentine's Day proponents and the diamond companies and I'm falling for it every day.

I am susceptible to advertising. I have to be careful because when I buy a magazine I might see an outfit and think, "If I had that outfit I might feel confident and put together and attractive." I bought clothes I never even wore because they weren't me. I am better at this now. I must be getting closer to peace with the real me and farther away from trying to create who I am new every year or season through clothes. But it's always a bit of a struggle.

The guys I was with were kind of like those wrong outfits. They would have been perfect for somebody but they didn't fit me. Since I didn't know me, I couldn't tell what fit me and what didn't. It took a few years of wearing that wrong relationship in my life before I would become so chafed by the bad fit that I couldn't stand it anymore and stripped it off. Then I was naked, and instead of walking through that experience, I quickly found another outfit to wear. Any outfit. The chance of that happening to fit, especially when I wasn't paying attention to my size, was probably impossible. But I couldn't stand to be out in the cold so I didn't know any other way to go.

If there is a Cupid who shoots you in the heart with an arrow so you fall in love, it would be nice if he'd do the rest of us a favor and shoot our hearts with a year's worth of novocain so our hearts would be numb and we wouldn't feel the lack of this kind of love in our lives.

I've been in lots of relationships, and at the time I thought I was in love but now I think it was something else that carried me away. And I guess the thing is, as long as I wanted to get away from me, I was susceptible to getting carried away.

## An Unexpected Chance

I met Dick on a cold January day at a Saturday morning meeting that I attended regularly for many years. It was a chance encounter during a time when I was making an extra effort to be friendly. I was determined to go on a date with someone before deciding they weren't for me. I thought maybe I was still single because I was too picky.

I didn't even really notice Dick until the end of the meeting when we chatted for a few minutes. He said he was from upstate New York, a rural area with lots of beautiful places to hike. I told him there were some nice places to hike and walk in my neck of the woods.

Dick called me the next day. We talked for a while about a bunch of nothing which I took as a good sign because that's not easy for me to do. I liked the sound of his voice. I didn't remember all that well what he looked like other than that he was a pretty big guy. I mentioned I liked movies, especially foreign films at my favorite movie theater in West Newton. He said he liked them too which I was surprised to hear because not too many people I know do. Slower readers can have a tough time with subtitles and it's just not everyone's cup of tea. He asked me out for lunch and a movie on the following Saturday. I said yes.

It turned out later that he really didn't like foreign films. I didn't realize it at the time, but I gave him a lot of information about myself before getting to know him. He used it to say he liked the same things I did. I would have been much better off to get to know him and see what he liked without telling him so much about what I wanted. I used to think I was very trusting and that's why I got involved with men so quickly. Now I see it wasn't trust but impatience. I didn't want to have to wait long enough to get to know them. It was a shortcut with only a slim chance of success. The real problem with this method wasn't that there was such a small chance of things working out though. It was the enormous cost if they didn't, but I wasn't remembering to treasure everything I had until I was in danger of losing it. My freedom, my life, and my son's life were all things I took for granted, not realizing jumping into a relationship too quickly had the potential to threaten them.

I was nervous when I met Dick again for the movie date, worried I wouldn't recognize him. But I did. He was a former Marine, over six feet tall, with very short, light colored hair and blue eyes. We went to an Italian restaurant next to the movie theater for lunch. I was going to order a salad in addition to my meal, but when I saw the look on his face because of the added expense, I changed my mind. I let him pay for dinner and the movie, a very unusual move for me. I remember how he fingered the bills as he took them from his old, worn wallet, carefully removing them to pay for the meal and the movie.

Afterwards we went to a quiet coffee shop and sat next to each other on a couch. Sitting next to him felt nice. I was tired, not just that day, but from life, from being a single working mom for a long time. I just wanted to lean up against somebody and get comfort. It felt nice to lean on him a little.

At the end of our first date, Dick said to me when I gave him a peck on the cheek goodbye, "Anything that happened before five minutes ago doesn't matter." I just loved that he said that, since I have a colorful past. A colorful past...that sounds like it should be a good thing, when actually it doesn't usually mean that at all, although I'm much more comfortable with the color than I used to be. I've been working hard on myself and my life and with God's help I've made a bit of progress. So the idea that what happened before today doesn't matter was music to my ears. Unfortunately, it wasn't something Dick was actually able to deliver on, although I'm sure he would have liked to.

We talked on the phone a few times. I realized that Dick didn't have much money. So for our next date,

I invited him over to my house to have dinner and watch a movie. My son came home at one point during the evening. Dick was lying on the couch. He said he was tired because he was working the night shift at that time. Ryan took an instant dislike to him, ostensibly because he was lying on the couch. I used to think if my son didn't like someone right away, I would pay attention. Instead, I made an excuse for Dick.

At the time I thought it was OK for Dick to lie down because he was tired. But when I think back on it, it would have been nicer to have a date with someone who wasn't broke and exhausted. When someone needs help, something inside me leaps to the surface, thinking "That's where I can come in handy." And I can. But it drains me, and makes the relationship uneven. I don't mean for it to be that way. I think it will just be temporary, and once they're feeling better, or well again, or back on their feet, I'll get support from them. The trouble is, I think by helping them, what I'm really doing is keeping them off their feet.

I invited Dick to sleep over that night, as he seemed very tired. I felt OK about it, because we didn't have sex that night. I think he interpreted my actions as more than what they were. I underplayed what I did as less significant than it was. I bought an extra muffin in case he stayed overnight. A friend of his told him that meant I knew I was going to invite him to stay. I didn't think that was true but maybe he was right. I was lonely.

I wasn't attracted to Dick as a boyfriend initially, although I liked him as a person, but I was trying to be open-minded by giving things a chance. I thought God put him in my life for a reason and that's probably true. I thought the reason was so I would finally have the long-term, committed relationship I always wanted. That might be kind of true. It turned out he helped me get over being so willing to think everyone I met might be the one. He helped me to not want to be in a relationship so much. He helped me to be much more careful. So maybe he was a necessary element on the path of my being in a long-term, committed relationship someday.

I always expect God's work in my life to be light as a feather, pleasant in every way and easy to take. But I might be such a tough case he practically has to drop a stone tablet on my head to get me to look up.

## Predictable Directions

The other day in my women's group meeting for victims of domestic violence we were asked by the group leader Debbie if there was anything that would have helped us to get out of the situation we were in more quickly. At first I couldn't think of anything, but then while I was listening to the others I thought perhaps if I had known that the little things I saw in the beginning were going to turn into big, bad things with near certainty, it might have helped. I probably thought somehow I knew what a domestic violence abuser looked like, and I would recognize him before I cared about him so much it was hard to let go. But just like alcoholics are not always unshaven homeless people in trench coats with their booze in paper bags clutched tightly to their chest, domestic violence abusers don't always start out looking like they are going to be so scary.

After the relationship ended, I found out at the counseling center that certain things are likely to be very bad signs, like extreme jealousy and being very controlling.

I found out after our first date that Dick smoked cigarettes. I quit smoking years before, so I was predisposed to avoid dating a smoker. Dick didn't smoke when we were on our first date. He cleaned his car before he picked me up so I wouldn't smell the smoke.

Within the first couple of months dating, we had an unpleasant disagreement. I told Dick I wanted him to leave my house. He didn't go. That turned out to be something that only got worse, never better. There were many nights that I was out in my car somewhere, unable to return to my own nice, warm home for which I paid the mortgage and the oil bill, because Dick was there and wouldn't leave. He threatened to let my dogs out into the street once when I was out and wouldn't come back. So I couldn't stay and I couldn't go and there's nowhere else. If I had known then that a behavior like that would inevitably become much worse perhaps I would have been able to end things back then. I just don't know.

A measure of my desperation to be in a relationship with somebody was my decision to try going to counseling with Dick after dating for a few months instead of just ending the relationship. I think embedded deep down inside me is an idea that a partner in life is evidence that I'm worthwhile, and therefore lack of one must mean I'm not. In this case being with Dick began deteriorating my feelings of self worth so I was actually moving in the wrong direction on this issue.

The first major sign that this relationship was not working was a disagreement over the Pledge of Allegiance. I love my country but I think the only allegiance I should pledge is to a higher power. Dick, a former Marine, listened to my sentiments about the pledge with a sneer of disgust. He put me down and attacked me and my beliefs, and I should have known right then and there it was going to be more trouble than I could handle.

I can see now, looking back on it, that neither of us was a fit for the other, but both of us wanted to have someone else in our lives, so we tried to make it fit. I thought God put Dick in my life so I would have someone around, not so I could realize we weren't a good fit. So when things didn't go well, instead of breaking up, I suggested counseling and Dick agreed to try it. Something in me needed to be in a relationship so badly that I was willing to go to almost any lengths to try to make it work.

Our first counselor was a guy in Holliston named Dennis. I went with high hopes that once we ironed out a few wrinkles, we could do alright. One of the first things he said to us is that our relationship was strong, but not stable, and that we had to work on stability. He encouraged Dick to let go a little. And he encouraged me to share my feelings more.

There was a little more trouble all the time. There was the time he smoked pot and didn't tell me. That doesn't sound like such a big deal to regular people maybe, but to the sober people I knew, sober usually meant drink and drug free. We were visiting a friend of his, and the two of them went off alone for a while. I don't remember how I figured out what they were doing. Maybe they were acting different, or maybe I could smell the pot. Dick admitted they were smoking pot, and then defended it as not necessary to mention to me and also not related to sobriety, defined as the freedom from alcohol.

Faced with his convictions I became doubtful of my own. Instead of focusing on the fact that he hid this from me, I focused more on his definition of sobriety. Even though everyone I knew counted abstinence from drugs as part of staying sober, I could also see the point of view that just not drinking could qualify as sobriety. The incident left me uneasy, but wasn't enough to cut all the hopeful heartstrings yet.

When we discussed what happened in counseling, our counselor Dennis said this could be a "deal-breaker." Dick was mad but he decided to quit smoking pot, so supposedly everything was OK. But I knew that was a pretty big lie of omission for a person in sobriety. He said he wasn't counting smoking pot as a staying sober item. But if that was the case, then he could have told me about it. For everything he hid – smoking cigarettes on our first date, smoking pot a few months later – the problem wasn't so much the activity as it was the hiding of it.

But I kept focusing on the activities instead of looking at the hiding. Dick was trying hard to change, and since I believe people can and do change, I continued to hope for the best.

Dick had a serious, potentially life threatening gastroenterological problem and needed surgery. His family was from upstate New York. He had nobody here to help him. I thought God would want me to help him, so I asked him to move in with me for a couple of months while he had surgery and then recovered.

The deal was supposed to be temporary – once he recovered he was supposed to move back out. But it took a whole extra year for that to happen. He argued that we wanted to live together someday anyway, so why not start while he was still here? And at first I said OK, instead of sticking to the original deal, even though I wasn't sure I wanted it.

One day we went to a friend's house. They analyzed our astrological charts for compatibility. The astrologer had said I had a sweet, naïve element to my nature, and that Dick had the potential to overshadow my element of sunshine with darkness.

I ended up with a headache before the end of the visit, and by the time we got home I felt terrible and went upstairs to lie down. Instead of being nice to me when I was sick, Dick was mean. I wasn't expecting that, as I had been so nice to him many times when he was sick.

My son was about 12 years old when Dick and I met. I thought sometimes about how it might be nice for Ryan to have another male role model in his life in addition to his Dad, and how it would be great if there were someone who could take him skiing or show him how to do things his Dad and I didn't know how to do.

At first, Dick seemed to be great with Ryan. He was interested in him, and began playing football in the backyard with a few of the kids. Dick would be what he called "the all-time quarterback", and he would let Ryan be the "all time receiver." But I could see signs of his temperament. He would get upset with some of the plays, just like a young kid. He took Ryan's side against me, to get on Ryan's good side. Yet he would criticize me for spoiling him. Before the relationship ended, he was in competition with Ryan, even though there was no competition. If Dick complained that I treated Ryan better or that Ryan was more important, I agreed. I told him Ryan is the most important person to me. There is no competing. I felt my son would always come first. I had trouble putting myself before Dick though.

## The Dreamer (part 1)

Out of touch with reality,
anyone can plainly see it
except her
She doesn't know yet
that it's a sure bet
her life is on the wrong track but
it's not too late to go back

Coming sure as day and night and
if she knew she'd be so frightened
She doesn't know yet
can't see the train wreck
because she's
trying too hard to live a dream
It's not too late to wake up

## Where Did I Go?

We were paying a lot of money out of our own pockets to see Dennis. Miracles were not happening because of it. So I tried to find another counselor to go to that would be covered under my insurance. That's how we ended up with our new counselor, Dr. Gareau.

I write in a journal many nights before I go to sleep. I bravely looked back through my first journal from the time I started going out with Dick, and ironically I see that he didn't like the way things went sometimes in the beginning of the relationship. He threatened to end it regularly in the first few months. Now when I read that I think, why didn't I just let him?

I was planning to read the rest of the journals to help me write about what happened, but I'm not sure it's a good idea anymore. I don't want to relive those times. They were so hard to go through the first time, so unbelievable. Sometimes I wrote down what Dick said verbatim. When I read those notes, I go back to what it was like with an immediacy that leaves me feeling queasy. Maybe re-reading some of my journals and writing about this contributed to the depression that I sank into this year.

In the beginning of our relationship I kept going back and forth on things. Sometimes I wanted to live together and/or get married someday. The rest of the time I was backing off of that position. Once I gave him a key and then I wanted it back. It's clear to me reading it now that I was torn between my old self and my new self. My old self was too impulsive, jumping right in over my head, assuming things would work out with little or no evidence. My new self was more cautious, realizing that just because I felt something in a given moment didn't mean I felt it for real or for long. After I would do something like give Dick a key to the house which I knew he would like I got a nagging feeling inside me letting me know it was not the right move for me.

My behavior probably exacerbated Dick's insecurities and we began a spiral down together. We went from each doing OK on our own to doing much worse together. Later, in counseling, Dr. Gareau would say a relationship is supposed to make things better, not worse, or what's the point?

I re-read part of M. Scott Peck's <u>The Road Less Traveled</u> recently, and he mentions something in his book that I think is true of me. It's something about how some people want to feel morally superior to other people, so they like being in the position to forgive them magnanimously. I think I felt like I wasn't good enough and I went out with people that I thought had even more problems than I did so by comparison I looked good.

I wanted a relationship so badly that I focused on how hard Dick was trying to change, and I minimized the bad things, like Dick's jealousy. To be fair, Dick tried harder to change than anyone I ever met. In his good moments, he could recognize what he was like in his bad moments, and he really didn't want to be like that. He went to counseling on his own, even before we started couples counseling. He voluntarily attended anger management classes, something I think most people do only when forced. He went to couples counseling, even though he was afraid the counselors would tell us it would be best if we split up. He took drugs recommended to him by the psychiatrist as possibly helpful to his condition, even though he didn't really want to take them. And he voluntarily went to the emergency room and then the mental health unit of a hospital for a few days when he was getting out of hand. But in spite of all his efforts, there were still too many problems for us to survive.

He started calling me names, saying I was having an affair. I wasn't, but that didn't stop Dick from accusing me of it, sometimes on a daily basis. For a long time I thought this would go away eventually because I wasn't actually seeing anyone else. But I was missing the boat entirely with that kind of thinking. Even though it was only happening in Dick's mind, the fact that it was in his mind was all that mattered, not whether or not it was really true. And because it was in his mind, there was no way for me to get it out.

When he would call me names and treat me badly, that behavior was very effective in cutting heartstrings left and right. But I guess by then I had a tangled mess of heartstrings, so it took a lot to cut through them all. And sometimes I could see a nicer Dick in there, wanting to prevail.

He came up with a little nickname for me – Munchmouse. This kept one little heartstring viable while the others were being cut clean through. When his behavior was bad it ripped me up, but I didn't let go right away. I would think of that little nickname. My heart would soften a little because I thought it was a sweet thing. I magnified this one small good thing into a really big size and minimized the many rotten things into a small pile. But once I was away from it all, I could see that one small good thing doesn't mean enough next to a mountain of rotten things.

When the fighting between us would start, I would tell Dick to leave my house. But he wouldn't go. Then I would try to leave the house to get away from him, but sometimes Dick would stop me. When I did get out, I often found myself outside my own house, in my car, not wanting to leave but feeling like I had to because Dick wouldn't. I felt homeless, even though I had a home. I was tired, but I couldn't go to bed. I would stay away, sometimes for a couple of hours, hoping that when I returned things had calmed down. But they often hadn't. I needed to get sleep so I could work, but when we were fighting, I couldn't. Dick would call me on my way to work, when I was at work and on my way home from work. There was no peace. And we were fighting more and more.

I asked lots of people – friends, people at work, people I met – about fighting. Everyone said it was normal and they fought too, so I didn't realize right away the kind of fighting we were doing might be much worse than other people's. Especially since I was sharing about it in counseling, and no one said yet the relationship was hopeless.

One guy I talked to asked me if there was any hitting going on, and I said no. But there were lots of other things going on short of hitting. At the time I didn't know they counted as domestic violence too.

In the beginning I would try to reason with Dick, addressing his accusations and explaining that they weren't true or why they didn't make sense. But that didn't work. After a while of his going at me with his insults and accusations, I would start screaming at him to leave me alone. I screamed so hard I would have to use sore throat spray to numb the pain in my throat so I could get to sleep.

I could see I was turning into someone I didn't like, but I didn't know how to stop. Dick wouldn't leave when I asked him to and wouldn't stay away when I said I didn't want to see him anymore. I was reluctant to involve the police in our altercations. I would threaten to call them if he didn't leave, but I didn't follow through.

I think Dick was able to stop just short of doing things that would have cut the heartstrings clean through sooner, like hitting me or having a big fight with me in front of my son. We seemed to have our major problems when my son was at his Dad's or when we were off together someplace.

The worst fights happened when my son was visiting his Dad. I think this is a place where God's grace protected my son. I think Ryan could have been affected much worse, although I think he was affected more than I like to admit.

I think Dick knew I drew the line at getting hit and fighting in front of Ryan. He managed to keep his behavior short of those two marks. I wish I had drawn the line a bit higher. If someone asked me ahead of time if I would put up with fanatical jealousy, disrespectful name calling, being driven out of my own home, etc., I would have easily answered, "No way. Absolutely not. Not a chance."

But once I was in the middle of it, I was so confused. For a long time I focused on how to change what was going on, not how to get away. I thought if I stood up for myself and said it was unacceptable, it would stop. But that didn't work. I had to be able to back it up with the action of leaving, and I guess I wasn't ready to do that for a while. I think partly because I thought God wanted something else and that if I were spiritual enough things would work out. But I'm not that spiritual. Maybe if God himself was in this relationship as the woman, she would have been able to calm the stormy seas by focusing on the good in Dick. But my attempts to do that failed utterly. I might have a bit of God in me, but not enough to accomplish that tall order.

My sister made a joke once and said I was able to take an employed man and turn him into an unemployed mess. But it wasn't that funny because I think it's kind of true. Dick quit his job after we began dating, and I tried to help him financially for a while.

Once Dick said he'd give me all his money and I could pay all his bills, give him a small amount of cash, and keep the rest. And I wondered, "What if there's not enough to cover the bills," which was indeed the case. I kept track of his money, but at the point where I had "lent" him one or two thousand dollars, I realized I don't have that kind of money myself and I stopped.

Maybe I'm trying to do for them what I wish someone would do for me. I'd be better off taking care of myself though, because the guys are not holding up their end of the bargain they know nothing about. I keep thinking God would want me to be kind to someone and take care of them. I think God does want me to be kind to someone and take care of them – me! When my first thought in a bad situation is what the consequences will be for Dick if I take care of myself, that's a bad sign. I thought I could take care of me and of him, and that if I helped to take care of him, he could pay me back by loving me and providing some companionship.

Sometimes I could feel the little quiet voice inside me when I did something I shouldn't have done, but the loud part of me was already talking. One time I bought Dick a shirt, and he was telling me not to do it, but I was insisting. The little quiet voice inside of me agreed with Dick, and I felt ill at ease. But I had already said I would buy the shirt, so I didn't put it back on the rack and say, "You're right. Never mind."

After Dick and I broke up, my sister tried to buy something for me that I thought I should buy for myself. She tried to insist because she has more money than me. And I didn't like that feeling at all. It is true that she has more money than me (mainly because she is much more careful with her money than I have been with mine), but it wasn't such a great feeling.

I could see Dick was struggling financially so I was trying to help. But I realize now he might have felt badly about himself because of it, like I did when my sister tried to help me. Multiply that by many little times and it probably got easier for him not to believe in himself and his own abilities. Helping him do things he needed to work out for himself might have been like a vote of no confidence. After all, he managed to struggle by before he met me.

Once when I got a bonus from work I bought Dick a kayak. A big example of something I did that I didn't need to do, especially since it was expensive and not a basic necessity. Some part of me felt like I had to share my good fortune with him because he wasn't getting any extra money from work. But the truth is I had lots of other things I could have better used the money for, since I'm not wealthy myself, even though I was better off financially than Dick. Just after agreeing to purchase it, Dick got a notice from the car loan company saying his car loan was behind. He got visibly upset when he opened the envelope, and I asked him what was wrong. He told me and I offered to let him return the kayak and use the money to get current on his car payments. But he refused. I looked at catching up on car payments as more important, but he probably felt the kayak was too good to pass up and that somehow he'd work out the car payments. That's not the decision I would have made which was another good reason I needed to financially separate myself from him. The incident went into the databank labeled "Maybe this isn't working out so well," joining lots of others.

One of the things that kept me with Dick longer than I meant to stay is the picture in my mind of him fingering his money so carefully on our first date. I didn't realize at the time how badly off he was in his money situation. I felt sad to think of him not having enough money to pay for things he needed. When I do this kind of thing, I'm forgetting to think about me. I don't really want to be someone's old wallet, my function being to provide some of my own limited dollars to pay their bills. I forget to remember that I work hard for my money, and it's OK for me to have some when someone else doesn't because there's a lot of things they could have chosen to do differently and didn't.

When it came to Dick's finances I could see the train coming down the tracks headed right for him, so to avert disaster I tried to push him out of the way before the train arrived. Maybe he would have jumped out of the way himself before the train got there, and now neither of us will ever know because of my interference. I was the only one who thought a train was coming when I was pushing, so instead of being happy I pushed him out of the way, he was just mad that I shoved him. Even if he were hit by the train he might have learned to be more careful on the tracks next time. All I taught him was that if I was around, I would watch for the train. After a while I don't want to watch for trains. I don't want to have to keep helping. I think he'll start seeing the train at the same time I do and step out of the way before I feel like I have to push him. And when that doesn't happen, I don't like it. But the answer could have just been if I let him watch for his own trains from the beginning, he'd either get hit or not, but either way it wouldn't have anything to do with me.

The biggest irony is that while I was busy watching out for the trains I thought might hit him, I was too busy to notice I was standing right in the middle of a different set of tracks myself. An enormous freight train was bearing down on me and I wasn't getting myself out of the way.

## The Concert

Dick and I didn't have the same taste in music. He liked southern rock and roll. I liked more current, alternative rock type music. I bought tickets to go to a concert in Boston to hear Susan Tedeschi sing, as I thought we both might enjoy it. It was a pretty big deal for me to go to a concert in Boston. I don't do it very often. We took the train into the heart of the city, then walked to the theater. In our seats, waiting for the show to start, Dick started in about something. I don't even remember what it was. He grabbed me by the arm, marching me out of the aisle and down the stairs, saying we were leaving. I managed to pull away and go into the ladies room. Lots of women were coming in and out, going to the bathroom before the show, looking happy and excited. I stood in the outer lobby looking at myself in the big mirror. I was pale and frightened looking and I thought to myself, "This can't be my life." When I came out, Dick grabbed me and tried to march me back, saying he changed his mind and we'd see the show after all.

But I said, "No, I'm going home." We began to attract the attention of the security guards at the door who were checking people as they entered the theatre. Dick realized it too, so before they came over to see what was going on, he quieted down and we left.

In the train on the way home I said over and over that I didn't want to see him anymore. He kept pleading with me, saying he was sorry and that I didn't mean what I was saying. I kept saying I did mean it. It was dark outside and the lights in the train made the windows into a dark mirror. I could see myself and Dick reflected in the glass, having a scene on the train in front of all the other passengers. The train rattled rhythmically down the tracks, the bass rumble coming up from under the train - clickety clack, clickety clack, matching the cadence of what was coming up from deep inside of me – this can't be my life, this can't be my life.

Unlike vampires who can't see themselves in a mirror, it seems I could only see the wreck I was becoming in a reflection - the ladies' room mirror at the concert hall or the darkened windows of the train.

But somehow after that train ride I agreed to keep trying for a while longer.

## Out on the Roof

One night when my son was out we were fighting again. It probably started in the usual way. He accused me of being unfaithful again which was a common theme. On this particular night, things got more out of hand than usual. When I tried to leave the house he blocked me from descending the stairs and getting out. He pinned me down on the stairs, but eventually let me go. I threatened to call the police if he wouldn't leave my house, but he knew I might not really do it. I dialed 911 this time though and when he realized I was actually calling he pulled the cord right out of the wall and the phone went dead. He went downstairs for a few minutes but I still couldn't get past him to get out the door. He worked himself up into even more of an insane rage than usual while he was downstairs and I got really scared. I heard him coming back up the stairs and my instinct took over. I had to get away. My heart was pounding, and I wasn't even thinking anymore. My whole body was tuned into one idea beyond just thinking. Move, move now, get away!

There is one narrow set of stairs that leads to the two bedrooms upstairs. The stairs lead directly into my room with no door to lock or hide behind. There are three windows in my room but all of them have a two story drop underneath. My son's room has a door on it but no lock. Two of his windows also have a two story drops but one of them leads out onto the roof of a small porch underneath. The only way I could get away was to go out the window and onto the roof. I pushed up the window and pulled out the screen as fast as I could. I had a couple of extra seconds, as Dick expected me to be in my room and didn't come towards Ryan's right away. My heart was pounding and adrenalin was pumping through me as I pushed myself out the small window in one fast, fluid motion, and crawled away from the window farther out onto the roof. If he tried to come out after me he'd have to go through the window too, but he was much bigger than I am. It would be harder for him to squeeze through. If he tried I could drop to the deck, and if I didn't hurt myself in the fall, try to run away.

It was cold out on the roof, dark and quieter. I felt better and safer now that I was out of the house, even though I am afraid of heights and normally wouldn't like being on that roof. I trembled as I clung to the roof, hugging the top tightly with my body flattened out against the sloping shingles.

A police cruiser pulled into my driveway silently, but with the blue lights flashing. The 911 call must have gone through just before Dick cut the cord and when the police couldn't reach me, they came to the house.

I could hear the policeman call for backup on the radio, saying into the static echoes "We've got one out on the roof." The way he said "one" was like "one nutcase" or "one crazy person" and I couldn't believe this was even my life or that I was really the one out on the roof.

As soon as Dick saw the blue lights he calmed right down and started begging me not to have him arrested. He sounded like a small child now, saying "Don't let them arrest me. Don't let them take me away."

When the police came in one officer took Dick outside to talk to him and the other talked to me inside. I was crying and crying, and I didn't want to look up. The officer was very nice to me and said this happens to lots of people. He also said he liked my two Golden Retrievers.

Dick told me before that he wanted to be a private investigator someday, and if he had a police record he wouldn't be able to get a gun permit or be an investigator. If he got arrested he might lose his job. I didn't want these bad things to happen to him, and I put that ahead of the bad things that were happening to me, right at that very moment.

I told the officers we had a fight and it was OK for Dick to stay if he promised to sleep downstairs on the couch and leave me alone. The officer offered me a temporary restraining order right there but I didn't take it. This amazes me now because I think it was my chance to break away and also because by not getting the restraining order I was giving Dick permission to behave that way, although I didn't see that yet. To get the restraining order meant to me that everything was over. There would be no more trying to make it work, no more counseling, no more talking, no nothing. I guess I wasn't ready for that yet. Also, I think I was in denial about how much danger I was in. Even though I had just felt so afraid that I jettisoned myself through the window onto the roof, I couldn't admit that Dick was really dangerous to me. I understood innately that as long as we were trying to work on the relationship, he had a motive to try to be nice to me. But as soon as I said we were done his motive for being nice would disappear completely. Even when he was trying hard to be nice he was pretty bad. I was afraid I wouldn't survive his wrath if I left him.

A couple of years later I got a copy of the police report. I felt very sad when I read that I told the policemen I felt safe. I didn't really feel safe with Dick, but I also didn't feel safe telling the police I didn't feel safe and getting a restraining order. It's a terrible place to be, feeling like there's no safe way out. No one could really protect me from Dick. A restraining order was just a piece of paper, and it wouldn't keep him away. So I said I wasn't afraid and they left.

Months later I did get a restraining order. Since it came to that in the end, I wondered if I could have saved myself a lot of agony by saying I wanted one the night I was on the roof. But I guess I wasn't ready. Maybe things went just as they needed to. Dick never did get to a place where he could let go, but maybe with all the counseling we went to and the medication he took between the roof incident and when we did break up, he got closer to that place where he could let go. Maybe if I left him on the roof day worse things would have happened to me. Maybe waiting worked.

## The Dog from the New Yorker

I read over my counseling notebooks. I noticed our first counselor Dennis was very supportive of us staying in the relationship. Our second counselor was too at first. But there came a point when the tide began to turn with our second counselor. Suggestions that we might not make it began. I can see now I wanted someone to tell me to leave and somehow make it safe to do it.

During one session, Dick had a fit of rage right in the counseling office. Dr. Gareau sent me out to the waiting room while he tried to deal with Dick. I flipped through an old copy of the New Yorker magazine. I found an article about a woman who took in a stray dog that sometimes for no apparent reason and with no warning, would turn vicious and bite her. But much of the time the dog was very sweet and she was softhearted. She tried everything – neighbor's advice, dog behavioral specialists - but after a couple of years with no significant improvement she eventually had to put the dog down.

It reminded me of my situation with Dick. He could be very sweet when he wasn't in a rageful fit, and that's part of what made it so hard to give up entirely on things. After Dick left Dr. Gareau talked to me about taking care of myself and being prepared to take whatever steps were necessary, including getting a restraining order to do it. I was so scared to take that step. Dr. Gareau confirmed what I already knew – it would be a dangerous time if we broke up because Dick would no longer have the incentive to try to have good behavior to save the relationship.

In our last summer together Dick broke down my front door in a fit of rage when I locked it to keep him out. I told Dick I didn't want to continue the relationship. He told me he could see there were a lot of problems but wanted me to give him one last chance. He promised that if he had any more bad behavior, we could just split up and he'd leave me alone. So I gave him one last chance, not expecting it to work out, but hoping it would mean the peaceful end of our relationship.

## Dance Lessons

I always wanted to learn to ballroom dance. I pictured it as a great way to keep the love alive as reality eroded the initial romance of a relationship. And in the early fall right before the end of our relationship as part of our final attempt to work things out, we signed up for lessons.

It was a disaster. Dancing with Dick was anything but romantic. He told me I was lucky he was willing to take dance lessons with me – most guys wouldn't dream of it. He didn't listen to the teacher or do what she said, and when I got confused and couldn't follow him he got mad at me. He said every mistake was my fault. It was the worst time, not romantic or fun at all.

## Change

In recovery, I learned that one of my character defects is expecting other people to change instead of me doing the changing. Most of the time I know I can't change other people. But I also know people can change and in this case Dick was trying very hard to do that. So I thought since I wasn't trying to change him it could work. But now I see that waiting for someone else to change because they're trying is still expecting other people to change. I might be able to afford the time, but I really can't afford the misery during the waiting period. Maybe Dick will change and it will be enough for someone else someday. But it wasn't going to work for us. More importantly, finally I changed by not trying to make it work anymore.

## Snap of the Last Heartstring

For a long time I was tied to Dick by what I think of as heartstrings. As the weight of our difficulties grew, the heartstrings began to break. But my heartstrings must be made of something pretty strong because it took a lot of weight before the last one snapped and I was free.

It's funny though, because even before that last heartstring snapped, somewhere along the line the truth became that even if things had gotten better from that point on, it was too late for the relationship to be saved. Enough time couldn't have passed in this lifetime to repair the damage that had already been done. After that, it was just a matter of accepting it was true and then navigating away as safely as possible.

Navigating away from a situation that became dangerous was very scary. Only the quiet voice inside me could help me then because there's no safe route to get away. I debated whether to ask for a restraining order many times. I made a few trips to the police station where I just sat in the parking lot. I made a couple of trips to the courthouse, and I asked about whether specific situations merited an order. I spoke with a policewoman one day. After she heard some of the things that were happening, she thought I would qualify for a protection order if I went to get one. But she also couldn't advise me to do it. She said sometimes things blew over without one, but sometimes delivery of a restraining order pushed people over the edge into the very violence I was wishing to avoid. So I kept hesitating, hoping he would stop.

I ended my relationship with Dick nearly three years after we first met. We went to counseling for almost our entire three-year relationship. I never knew anyone who tried as hard as Dick to change. In his good moments he could see what he was like in his bad moments and he desperately wanted to change. But I am the one who needed to change. I needed to change into someone who could value and take care of herself first. I needed to let go of the idea that being in a relationship meant I was valuable and believe I was valuable all by myself.

## The End

Dick asked if he could take me out to breakfast for my birthday in November. I didn't want to go because I was working on a project that was very important to me. I was going through a book I had put together with lots of information on the project. Dick didn't like me working on the project instead of going to breakfast with him, so he took the book with all the information it had taken me years to collect, and tore it up. Then he went out in the driveway and kicked my car, putting a big dent in the rear panel.

That was the incident that ended his one last chance. I told him it was over. He called me incessantly during the month of December. I hoped it would stop once he realized I wasn't going to change my mind. That didn't happen quickly. I had given him so many second chances he probably thought he could get yet one more.

## After the Break Up

Every year since my Mom died I invited my family to come for a get together at my house at Christmas. Dick said if I had my party he'd come to my house, throw a rock through the window, and beat the first person to come out the front door with a baseball bat. I canceled the plans for Christmas at my house.

Dick threatened to cause trouble at the Saturday morning meeting I normally attended if I tried to go there again. He came to my house and screamed in through the front window that there would be trouble if I went. So I stopped going to my regular meeting which is a consequence I never imagined as the result of a failed relationship. I went to a meeting in another program instead, trusting God doesn't care which meeting I attend.

I changed my home phone number to an unlisted, non-published number. I changed my cell phone number. I hoped this would be enough, that he would stop calling and threatening me without getting a restraining order.

One day in January, he left me a message that said, "You don't seem to be afraid of me enough anymore. So I am going to go after your son." Then I knew I had to try something different. I went down to the courthouse the next morning and asked for a restraining order. I was granted a temporary order, but I had to return to court two days later when Dick could also be there to tell his side of the story.

Dick tried to discredit me. I told the Judge I still had some of the phone messages Dick left, and invited him to listen to them if he'd like. The Judge granted the restraining order for both Ryan and me. The court advocate went with me in front of the judge and advised me afterwards to be careful. She told me about a counseling program I was eligible to go to free of charge. I went, and it really helped.

I was at rock bottom of my self esteem. I felt like I let this happen to me, and if I had been smarter or something I could have avoided it. But counseling helped me to see that this kind of thing could happen to anyone and does happen to a lot of people in all walks of life. Even though I stayed for three years which seemed like a very long time to me, some people stay even longer. It was good I got out when I did. Some people never make it out.

I joined the weekly women's group at the counseling center. The meetings were run by the domestic violence program Director. I met other women who were in scary situations similar to mine. The Director always said to me when I left the meetings, be careful and stay safe. Sometimes the other women's stories seemed really awful to me, but at the end of the meeting it was me she would single me out to say "be careful and stay safe." That's when I began to get an idea of how serious my situation really was.

Dick violated the restraining order many times. He called me multiple times at work. His telephone number would come up so I realized who was calling and didn't answer. He left messages. At first I was afraid to report it to the police and he kept saying he wouldn't call again so I hoped I wouldn't have to. When I went to my women's group meeting, they provided a lot of encouragement for me to report it. Women there were going through the same thing that I was, or worse. He kept calling, and finally after about the seventh time in a couple of weeks, I reported it. I didn't even know which police department to call. I tried the one in the town where he lived, and they told me to call the one in the town where I received the calls, so I did. I went to the station and waited for someone to take my statement. The officer asked me why I hadn't reported the violations right away, and I realized my hesitation wasn't helping my cause. I was able to harden my heart a bit after that and report all future violations immediately. Dick was arrested for violating the restraining order.

I had hesitated to change my work telephone number because I didn't want anyone there to know what was going on, but finally I told my boss what was happening and got a different telephone number. I stopped getting calls at work.

But then Dick started calling my ex-husband Phil and asking about me. Over the summer I got an unsigned note in Dick's handwriting saying he heard my dog died and he was sorry. I figured he found out from Phil. I was upset that he knew I didn't have a dog anymore. I brought the note to the police. Although I brought them a copy of a note Dick had written to me before we broke up on the same kind of paper in the same handwriting, the police said they couldn't pursue it because they didn't have the funding for a handwriting expert. They did call Dick to ask him if he sent the note. He said no. One of the officers suggested I get another dog as soon as possible, and I adopted my new dog the following month.

I began getting calls on my cell phone, from a restricted number. I received as many as nine calls within a ten minute period. I knew it must be Dick. Somehow he got my cell phone number. I reported it to the police but they couldn't prove the calls were from Dick even with the phone records.

At first the police maintained the possibility that perhaps Dick didn't have my cell phone number and the calls were from someone else. But then Dick had his young son call me and leave me a message. It wasn't a violation of the restraining order because Dick himself didn't speak, but it did prove he had my cell phone number.

In the meantime Dick's case for violating the restraining order by calling me at work came to court. I was told by the District Attorney's office Dick was given the option to attend a batterer's program or go to jail. At first he told the Judge he wouldn't attend the batterer's program. The Judge gave him a couple of days to think about it. He changed his mind.

The calls to my cell phone dwindled off in November. In January, one year after getting my restraining order, I went back to court to have it renewed. I brought documentation with me to show the Judge why I still needed the order, but he didn't even ask me for it. He had some kind of documentation of his own he reviewed, perhaps the police and court records on the case. The Judge asked me if I wanted to renew it for another year or make it permanent. I chose permanent, based on advice I got from my women's group, hoping Dick would take that as a message that things between us were over forever.

When Dick was informed, he called me on my cell phone and spoke to me, violating the order yet again.

He said he didn't expect me to make it permanent. I told him I couldn't talk to him, hung up the phone, and reported the violation to the police.

I have had some additional calls from a restricted number since. I get fewer calls, and they are less frequent. I am hopeful one day they'll stop entirely.

## A Prayer Answered

I've been thinking lately that maybe the difference between me and some people is that I didn't watch the shark swim around for long before I dove in and started swimming. Maybe if I had taken my time, I might have seen this wasn't going to work out. Maybe after this experience I will be able to take my time.

Maybe Dick really was the answer to a prayer. I thought the answer to my prayer would be a relationship where things worked out. But maybe what God thought I needed was a bit more discrimination in choosing who I spend my time with. Or maybe God thought I had to be broken of this need to have a guy in my life all the time, because since Dick and I broke up, I have not felt the same desire to be in a long-term, committed relationship.

It took more than a year of having the restraining order in place and Dick violating it many times until I had the energy to do more than just walk through each day and breathe. I was shell shocked for a long time after the stormy bitter end of our relationship and the frightening weather continued as Dick called despite the restraining order. I had strange, scary dreams. Once I dreamed that I was back at UMass where I went to college when I was young, and someone let lions and tigers loose all over the campus. I was out walking around among them and it was supposed to help me overcome my fear, but I was crazy afraid.

It's been about three years since Dick and I broke up. I still go to the women's group sometimes, although not every week. I feel safer now that there's some distance in time from the scariness, but I still lock my door all the time and try to be watchful when I'm out, especially when I'm walking my dog by myself. I hope he has moved on and never thinks of me but I doubt that's true since I still sometimes get calls.

I go to different meetings now. I don't want to go to any he might attend. I know the restraining order is supposed to mean he can't be where I am, and I can still go where I want, but I just think it's probably better if I am as invisible as possible. And I don't want an incident with Dick to disrupt the meetings for everyone else there.

I don't want to meet anyone new, at least not yet. I haven't spent any money on books about relationships. I haven't purchased any clothes to wear on a date. I used to do that sometimes before I met Dick. I don't want to put myself or my son in harm's way again. I'm scared. Maybe that kind of thing just isn't what's meant for my life, at least not right now.

The Dreamer (part 2)

Back in touch with reality,
only she can plainly see it -
what could be
Knows the time is now,
can clearly see how
 She needs to make her dreams come true
Just not the ones for two

Rising up from deep inside her,
dusty dreams to recreate her
Maps to the unknown
to somewhere she belongs,
now that she
reaches for a different dream
There's still time to live it now

## Determination to Fulfill a Dream

I denied the danger I lived in while I was in the midst of it, convincing myself that Dick would never do anything really bad.  Otherwise, how could I forgive and try again?  How could I sleep at night in the same room?  But once I got a little distance away from the situation, I realized I didn't know what he might or might not do.  I doubt if other domestic violence victims think their significant others would kill them, but it happens.  And so, although I don't think Dick would kill me, I can't be sure under the wrong circumstances he wouldn't.

I was pretty scared in trying to get away, that I might be creating those wrong circumstances.  But the good news about being afraid for my life is that I realized I don't have time to put my little dreams on the back burner anymore.  And whatever I'm afraid of in trying to live those dreams is unlikely to be worse than what I already made it through.

My fears are often in the wrong place. I was afraid I wouldn't be in another relationship before I met Dick but it was the relationship I should have been afraid of. I was afraid the relationship wouldn't work out when it was the best thing for me that it didn't. I am afraid of dying when what I should be scared of is that I'm not living my life.

My big dream was to get married and live happily ever after. While in pursuit of that dream, I ignored smaller, more personal dreams.

My sister saw a program on public television where Dr. Christiane Northrup suggested women sometimes get lost and tired and confused in all the roles they learn to do. To figure out what they want, she suggested they look back to what they wanted when they were about twelve years old.

When I was that age, I wanted to be a writer who lived in a house on the beach and drove a white sports car. I also wanted to travel to France. I'm not sure how I acquired the desire. It may have been because I took French from third grade through high school, so it seemed the most likely exotic destination. Or it may have been because my Mom let my French pen pal come to visit for a month during the summer when I was in the seventh grade. I was supposed to go to France to stay with her family sometime later but that never happened. Maybe it was because somewhere there is a little French blood running through the veins – my grandmother on my father's side had the last name of Chateauneuf.

Whatever the reason, I had visiting France tucked away in my back pocket as a dream I would fulfill someday.

Trip to Ireland

After Dick and I broke up I really needed to get away. I asked my sister if she'd like to go on a trip together. She didn't really want to go to France, but she would consider a cruise, or a trip to Ireland. Our grandfather emigrated from Ireland to America when he was a teenager, so we have some history there. I didn't really want to go on a cruise, so we went to Ireland.

My sister and I each had a girlfriend who wanted to join us, so the four of us took a week long tour of southern Ireland. Our tour group was relatively large, as we had a full size bus of people. It was wonderful, but a bit hectic. Up early every day, suitcases in the hotel hallway in the early morning and a different hotel nearly every night. The pace was perfect for my sister who has a higher energy level than I do. She likes to see as much as possible on a trip, especially historical sites.

But I'm not much of a history buff and my favorite time was when we had a few hours of free time, once in a lovely formal garden across from a set of stores, and another time when we could roam Dublin for the afternoon.  I split off from my sister and our friends and wandered around the main part of Dublin, walking through St. Steven's green on one of the rare sunny days of our trip, enjoying a bit of shopping.  I loved listening to the Irish accents of the women in the changing room at the department store, as they debated the merits of their selections.  Afterward, I went to the bottom floor where there was a food store.  I bought some kind of soft, chewy licorice candy that's not sold where I live.  I preferred these activities to a tour of a church or a museum.

While the others went to a nighttime show that was included as part of the tour, one night I went by myself to a more modern performance of an Irish show that happened to be playing at the hotel.  When I was buying my single ticket at the front desk, the young Irish woman helping me said, "Sometimes the best company is your own."  In her brogue, it sounded so comfortable, like I could even believe sometimes my best company could be myself.

While I was waiting in line for the doors of the theater to open, a French woman struck up a conversation with me.  She told me I looked like someone who would speak more than one language.  It was the best compliment!  I was thrilled she thought I looked a bit European.  My French was very rusty, but I used a bit of it and she used a bit of English and we managed just fine. Maybe I could fit in if I went to visit France.

I sometimes read Emmet Foxx for spiritual inspiration. One of his short essays is about a boy who goes to the circus. The one thing he wants to see the most is a tiger. While he's there, he sees clowns and elephants and trapeze artists, but he does not see the tiger. Emmet Foxx says, "Make sure you see the tiger." When it comes to travel, southern France is my tiger.

## The Soap Lady

I met the soap lady when she came to my workplace to sell her wares. As I browsed through her various soaps and sprigs of dried lavender, she told me that the lavender came from France. I mentioned I had always wanted to go and she told me about the tour she went on, run by a couple of Australians. I asked her a bit about the details, expressing my hope that someday I could do something similar. Although she never returned to my workplace again, I liked the soap she sold so much that I became a regular customer, ordering refills over the Internet when my supply got low.

My one and only life was going by and I spent too much of it trying to make hopeless relationships work instead of cutting loose and going it alone. I was scared to go to France alone. What about potential terrorists? What about the language thing? Or being disliked because I'm American? What about flying? The plane might crash. It was a lot of money to spend on something that would only last a week.

But would any of the potential scary men I might encounter be any scarier than the one I knew here? Would being unable to speak the language be any worse than not using my voice or losing it? Wasn't the chance of dying in a plane crash more remote than the possibility of dying here? Would the trip really only last a week or would the experience of going stay with me in a good way for the rest of my life?

It was time to let go of the big dream of living happily ever after and make some little dreams come true.

In the fall of 2005, the soap lady sent a message out to all her soap customers, announcing that the tour of France was on for this year, asking if anyone wanted to go. My immediate thought was "Yes," followed by "I doubt if I can afford it." So I put it out of my mind. But in the winter of 2006, I thought to myself, "To hell with it. Even if I can't afford to do any home repairs, etc. I want to go on a trip to France." I thought of writing the soap lady and asking if anyone had per chance cancelled, opening up a spot. Within a day or two, she sent out a letter saying there were still a couple of openings for the tour. I considered it a sign from God and wrote back immediately saying, "Sign me up!"

The thought of going to France alone was daunting to me. But joining a tour group sounded much less scary. At least I would be associated with a group even if I wasn't actually with anyone. They would plan where to go and do the driving, so I wouldn't have to worry about getting lost or deciding what to see. The couple who ran the tour were native Australians, which meant they spoke English. So even though I could practice my French, I would be able to converse easily in English if I needed to. And although I had only met the soap lady in person a couple of times over the past few years when I saw her at a craft or garden show, I was at least slightly acquainted with her and she was very pleasant.

Once I decided to go, the soap lady asked me if I'd like to share a room to save on the cost of the trip. Although I had planned to pay the extra money for a single room, I agreed, thinking I would use the money I saved as spending money for the trip. I was a little nervous about sharing a room with someone I didn't know well, but I've had several roommates over the years. I've even slept in a dorm type room at a yoga center with 10 women in 5 bunk beds all in one room. I was more worried about getting Euros, speaking French and flying than I was about sharing a room. I optimistically thought it would probably work out and tried not to worry about it too much.

## The Tour

The tour was advertised as a relatively intimate gathering of free spirits for a leisurely paced vacation which sounded perfect to me. The couple who ran the tour, Jim and Robbi, went through Italy, Turkey and France over a period of a couple of months or so. The tour my soap lady chose was at the end of May. It was called "Flavours of Provence."

The itinerary sounded delightful. I reveled in the village names and in the idea of leisurely lunches, fabulous French food, shopping on market day, and speaking French. I marked down on my calendar the different towns/villages I'd be in each day.

The focus of the tour was great food and fine wine. Since I don't drink, I wouldn't be partaking in the fine wine part, but I figured I could sit outside in the sun and wait for the others while they were busy in the wine tasting cave. I told them in the information I sent them about myself that I didn't drink alcohol. It may have seemed a bit strange to them that I was joining a tour where the price included some expensive fine wine, but I wanted to go on this tour and was willing to pay the price and ride out the awkwardness associated with declining the wines when offered.

Every time I told someone I was traveling to France they assumed Paris. I thought about extending my stay to include that famous city of lights but decided the extra stress wasn't worth it. The only things I would have really wanted to do in Paris – sit at a sidewalk café, eat great food and enjoy the ambience – I could do in Provence. I also like to shop, but my budget and social experience were more cut out for market day than famous Parisienne shops. Some people would say, "If you're going to France, you have to see Paris." But I decided to be nice enough to myself to do what I wanted to do and not what some people say I must. Provence was calling to me, not Paris, so I kept my plans limited to the tour.

I spent the next few months getting ready for the trip. I didn't want to look or sound like the stereotypical self-centered American tourist. I wanted to make every effort to blend, in my clothes and in my speech. I bought a set of French lesson CDs, to help me brush up on my very rusty French. I practiced my French by listening to CDs on my commute to and from work. I looked up the translation for the phrase, "thank you but I don't drink alcohol," just in case I needed it.

I had two heavy, old suitcases I got when I was in college. Neither was large enough alone to carry my week's worth of clothes. We were requested to bring only one reasonably sized suitcase on the trip so I bought a new suitcase. It was a beautiful blue lightweight suitcase with deep rose piping around the edges and a blue and white striped lining. I began planning what I would need to pack. I spent months figuring out what I could wear every day, determining what I needed to buy. The hours and hours I spent thinking of what combinations of clothes to pack so I would have exactly the right amount and the right kind of things to wear were the most enjoyable part of my days. I would do it at night, before I went to sleep, sketching the outfits and crossing out/adding different T-shirts and sweaters. I read the French only wear sneakers when working out, not when walking around, and that they don't wear shorts so I decided to leave my sneakers and shorts at home.

I get a little nervous about flying. I can do it, but I don't like it much. Sometimes I picture the plane crashing out of control into the sea which is not the kind of comforting thought I can drift off to in my window seat. So I outdid myself with audacity and asked my doctor for something to help me relax on the flight. She gave me two Adavan for the trip over and two for the trip back so I could stay calm and relaxed during my flight. I added some over the counter motion sickness medicine, and stashed it all away until it was time for my big trip.

## The Trip to France

My best friend Ria brought me to the airport. She's been my best friend for about fifteen years now and knows me better than anyone else. Before I got sober I had friends, but I was more apt to try to please them and less apt to be true to myself, so I'm not so sure who they got to know. After I got sober I realized I did a lot of things to please other people or out of fear of other people's opinions, but I didn't like myself. I began to stand up for myself sometimes which was very difficult but well worth it. I think how I feel about myself is in direct proportion to saying and doing what I have to say and do to be true to myself while being as kind to others as possible. So this is the person Ria got to know – the real me, as much as I even know who that is. She was kind enough to offer to bring me to the airport which was very calming to me. We stopped for coffee/tea and some

Dunkin Munchkins on the way into Boston, and I enjoyed the pleasure of her company until it was time to hop out of the car at the airport terminal.

I felt a sense of adventure that only surfaces once in a while in my relatively mundane life. After doing the same things day after day, I forget it might even be worth it to try to do anything else. The hassles associated with doing anything different, along with the expense, frequently preclude me from making big plans.

But that adventurous sense makes me feel that I'm more alive. I'm about to do something different, something that I might really like. Something that is not just living the same way day after day, liking it OK but not necessarily loving it.

I settled in for a long wait once I checked my bag at the airport. There was a kiosk selling noise canceling headphones, and I bought a small pair. The woman who sold them said if I didn't like them, I could return them on my way back through the airport a week later. But I did like them, especially while on the plane. I thought noise canceling headphones would cancel out all other sounds, but I was wrong. I could still hear voices of people talking to me. And I played with the canceling function, turning it on and off again so I could hear the difference it made with the large underlying sound the jet engines made. I'd like to have had some special noise canceling headphones that could have cancelled out just the noise Dick made.

I settled into my window seat. I don't usually care much for airplane food but this was better than most. There were both English and French movies to watch, and the French ones had subtitles available. The little pill I took so I wouldn't be nervous flying seemed to be working just fine.

I thought when we landed at the Paris airport where I would catch my connecting flight to Marseille, I would be able to see the Eiffel Tower. But Paris was nowhere in sight. The airport must be well outside the city.

The connecting flight to Marseille was leaving soon after the plane landed, so the airline rushed those of us who needed to catch it onto a special vehicle that drove around the outside of the airport, closer to where the smaller plane was loading up. We made a mad dash through the people clogged airport, trying to follow the lead man. I was concerned about a woman with a little boy who was bringing up the rear but everyone made it.

The flight to Marseilles was much shorter. It was bright morning now and I was excited to be so close to Provence. I talked a bit with a woman on the plane who lived near the airport, and she recommended I do two things while in Marseilles – take a tour of the Mediterranean by sea, and visit Notre Dame de la Guarde. Since I would only be there for one day and since I was very tired from lack of sleep (not much on the plane combined with the loss of 5 hours or so in the time difference), I doubted I would get to do either. But I thanked her for her thoughtfulness.

Once the plane landed I picked up my bags and walked out to catch a taxi. I said in French, "Good morning. I would like to go to the Mercure Marseilles hotel please." And the taxi man said, "There are several Mercure Marseilles hotels – which one?" I was unprepared for that question and quickly searched through my bag, trying to find the reservation confirmation with the address.

"Ah, yes. The Mercure Marseille in Old Port, " he directed the taxi driver, and I folded myself into the backseat of the cab. Apparently it gets hot early in Provence or the driver hadn't taken a shower too recently, because the aroma was a bit pungent. But I opened my window a bit and tried to enjoy the ride. The roads we took were not the most scenic, and the ride was longer and more expensive than I expected.

Fifty Euro later I was at the door of the quaint old hotel. The first thing I noticed was the outfit worn by the girls who worked behind the desk. They had on burgundy shirts or jackets, and on one shoulder, looped through a tiny loop at the top of the sleeve, was a beautiful multicolor pink and burgundy scarf, tied in a big bow. I never saw anything similar back home, and I just loved the way it looked.

It was about 9 AM local time. I was hoping my room would be ready early by some lucky chance so I could take a nap, but it wasn't. They suggested I try again around noontime. I asked if they could hold my bags while I walked around the city for a while. My first idea was to do a bit of shopping but all the stores were closed because it was Sunday. When I was little that was true in New England as well, but over the years things have changed and now almost all the stores are open on Sundays. So I didn't realize arriving on Sunday precluded shopping.

I ventured out to take a look around while I waited for check-in time. The first thing I saw on the side street leading away from the port was a carousel. It wasn't running on Sunday morning, but sat quietly, its gold trimmed splendor announcing that a bit of fun could be had in that pocket of the street. The carousel was two-tier, something I didn't remember seeing back home.

I like to ride the merry-go-round. They kept the carousel at the old amusement park at Nantasket Beach even after they tore the roller coaster and other attractions down. I've driven the couple of hours to bring my son there when he was little. We've been to another at Roger Williams Park and Zoo in Rhode Island. I was happy to see the familiar sight of my favorite children's ride first thing upon my arrival.

I had imagined I would be looking out at the Mediterranean Sea since I reserved a room with a water view. But the hotel was on the edge of the port, which was just a lovely basin. It undoubtedly kept the worst of stormy weather away from the fishing boats but afforded no view of the open sea. On one side of the basin, steep narrow streets with rows of concrete buildings led to a point high above the bay where a white building glittered on top in the sunlight.

All along the port booths were set up and people were selling fish (many still alive, in blue plastic basins), food, knives, articles of clothing, and toilet paper roll holders that made noises like crickets (apparently a Provencal thing). I strolled around the semi-circle of the port basin and back being careful to keep my valuables close to me in case I looked like an easy mark to a thief. I saw some pareos – large square pieces of cloth that could be tied around the waist like a skirt, frequently worn over bathing suits. I decided to think about it before buying anything, especially since I would have to carry it with me as I walked around. I had never used a pareo, but it seemed like a good idea.

To pass the time, I started walking up a hill away from the port. When I saw a sign for Notre Dame de la Guarde, I remembered the recommendation of the woman I met on the plane and I headed in that direction.

I walked up and up, trying to remember the names of the streets I was on – Rue de Breteil, turn onto Rue de Dragon – up and up and up. I tried to remember some of the shops I was passing – a butcher, two shops that sold fruits and vegetables, some boulangeries and patisseries. I passed by a small terraced paved park for children with benches for parents to sit. A man practiced soccer with his son.

Lots of people walked their dogs in the city, but there was no good place for them to go to the bathroom. The people must have been really good about cleaning up after the dogs since I didn't see much evidence to the contrary.

The streets were narrow with tiny cars parked on both sides and a tiny aisle in between, big enough for one car only. The buildings were four or five stories high. People had clotheslines strung between their windows with a few colorful items hanging in the sun against the peach stone of the walls.

I asked a friendly woman for directions, and in French she told me to go straight, take a left, then a right, and go up some stairs. I understood her! And I kept going up five flights of short steep stairs with iron railings connecting the street below with the street above for pedestrians. I slowly climbed up the long, terraced stairs, watching tour buses and cars driving up the steep hill on the road beside me. Then more stairs, but I was getting closer to the cathedral.

At one point I thought, "It's a good thing I didn't wait any longer to make this trip. I don't know if I could do it if I were any older." I wasn't sure I'd make it now. My heart was definitely getting an aerobic workout. I could easily see now how French women stay so thin.

I reached the bottom of the cathedral - more stairs and more stairs, but I was so close I would not stop now. My legs were leaden and my feet were beginning to hurt. I was working up a sweat – luckily I had a tank top on and had taken my jacket off and tied it around my waist. But no sunscreen – it was in my suitcase.

Once I finally got to the top and inside the cathedral, I thanked God that I didn't have heart failure on the steep, long walk up, and asked for help to find my way back down. Then I looked around. The cathedral had gorgeous painted ceilings, and it was a lovely old stone church with dark wooden benches and glowing stained glass windows.

I stepped out onto the stone patio that surrounds the cathedral and it was all worth it. What a magnificent view! Clusters of bleached stone houses with red tile roofs dotted the side of the hill that sloped steeply down to a glass blue Mediterranean sea dotted with tiny white sails, lightening to a softer shade of blue at the horizon.

There was a gentle breeze. I could also see down to the area where my hotel was located. I had climbed a long way. At least the return trip would be downhill. I lingered up on the patio surrounding the church for a little while, soaking in the scenery, taking some pictures and resting.

On the way out I stopped at the gift shop. I didn't really want to have to carry anything back down the hill with me, and even as I was buying it I knew this was the kind of thing I would probably rarely use, but I purchased a book on Provence, illustrated with pencil type drawings and providing a bit of information on various things Provencal.

I made my way back down the hill, retracing my steps, trying to remember if I'd passed the things on my way up that I was now passing on my way down. Eventually I arrived back at the hotel hoping my room would be ready and I could finally lie down. But it was still not ready yet. So I went upstairs to the hotel bar which was practically empty. Another woman sat by herself at a table. I selected a table near the window and sat down. The bartender came over to ask me what I'd like. I ordered a glass of ice tea and began leafing through my new book.

A few minutes later he brought over a cup of tea in a glass mug with a lime wedge, and what looked like a giant salt shaker (but it was filled with sugar). I asked in French if it was sugar and he said yes. Then I tried to say in French that it looked like a big salt shaker to me. The woman at the other table said to me in English, with a somewhat contemptuous look, "You want salt for your ice tea?" I explained in English that I'd never seen anything like that before. She said I mustn't have seen much of Europe which was true but I realized I didn't need to make a show of it.

Ignoring the woman, I lingered over my slightly cool tea with the lime and sugar, but finally decided to go back to the lobby and see if my room was ready. I brought my empty ice tea glass and the sugar shaker to the bartender and asked him "Combien ca coute?" or "How much does this cost?"

Instead of answering me with a price he started explaining to me that I didn't have to clear the table, that it was his job. At first I thought he was trying to tell me I could have the ice tea for nothing but luckily I didn't walk away because then he took the money for it.

Feeling like I barely averted another Americanized misunderstanding, I headed back toward the lobby hoping to be quiet and talk to no one and do nothing else until my room was ready. I was getting exhausted and trying to speak and understand French would be tiring even if I had a good night's sleep the night before.

I sat down in the lobby to wait. Despite my best efforts, I fell asleep in the chair. I kept waking myself up with my own snoring and then falling back to sleep again. Finally, my room was ready about 3 p.m., and the porter brought me upstairs. Once I began snoring in the lobby, they may have prioritized me.

The room was very lovely. The two windows overlooked the main street below and just across the street was the fish pier. I opened them both to let in some fresh air. The vendors were still set up, but I was too tired to go back to buy the pareo I had seen earlier. I laid down on the bed and promptly fell asleep.

I woke up a couple of hours later to the sound of music in the street and lots of horns beeping. Maybe someone got married. I woke up groggily. I remembered the advice of some seasoned travelers, which was to take no more than a two hour nap and then get up and go to dinner. So I got up, got dressed, and took a walk over to a restaurant in the square I noticed earlier on my way up to Notre Dame de la Guarde.

## Dinner in Marseilles

I selected my restaurant based on two factors – it had tables outside (as did most all of the restaurants around the bay, even McDonald's), and it had beautiful deep blue glass plates in the shape of a leaf sitting on top of crisp white tablecloths.

The menu was set up under an umbrella, in front of the tables on the sidewalk so prospective diners could peruse it at their leisure, in the shade. After I was seated and had ordered an Orangina to drink, I watched a man studying the menu. He wore a turtleneck sweater, had longish hair, and seemed very European to me. He took his time looking at the menu which is something I hadn't thought to do before I went in.

My normal method of eating out is to order some food at whatever restaurant I'm at, eat it very quickly, and leave as soon as possible, freeing up the table for some other guest. I wanted to slow down and do things the way the natives would do them. So I relaxed in my chair, willing myself to enjoy a leisurely pace of choosing my meal and eating it.

All around me I could hear other diners talking to each other, mostly in French. It was music to my ears. I loved listening to the accents and inflections so foreign to me. I didn't understand their conversations, and I could only communicate minimally with my waitress. But I found minimally was quite enough to order food, let them know I enjoyed my meal, and pay the bill. And that was really all I needed to be able to do.

Back at home, when I go out with people, I tend to overcompensate for my somewhat shy nature by talking a lot, telling stories and asking questions, giving myself a damn headache. Here, I could understand little and communicate less, and it was relaxing.

I ordered the salad Nicoise and some broiled scallops because I was too afraid to try the bouillabaisse, which I think was the house specialty. It turned out that as soon as I ordered food, they took the blue glass leaf plate away and brought the food on plain white practical plates. I guess the leaf plates were for the look of the table only and not for eating on. That's something I've never bothered with, but I could see the advantage to a beautifully set table, as that was what drew me to the restaurant in the first place.

After dinner I walked back to the hotel, and got a good night's sleep before setting out in the morning to meet up with the tour group.

## The Point de Reconnaitre

I took a taxi back to the Marseille airport, leaving plenty of time so I would not be late to meet with the group. I found the Point de Reconnaitre in the terminal I arrived in and sat down an hour ahead of schedule. But by 5 minutes to 1:00, our appointed meeting time I knew something must be wrong. No one else from the group was there. I asked the girl at the desk and found out that there was another Point de Reconnaitre in the other terminal, for international flights which is where I was supposed to be and where I happily found the group.

There were 15 people on the tour besides the lovely couple who run it, Jim and Robbie, and the extra person they brought to help them drive, Doug. The number was limited by how many will fit in the two mini-vans they use to drive us around. It was easier to get to know everyone a little bit in the relatively small group compared to the busload we had when I went to Ireland.

There were 5 couples and 5 singles, about half from Australia and the other half from the United States. Introductions were made all the way around, I made a quick trip to the ladies room, and then off we went in two mini-vans. The first stop was a lavender museum.

Once we got to the museum I went to the ladies room again with a couple of other women on the tour. One of them stepped into the next available bathroom and exclaimed, "Oh my God. This is one where you pee standing up." I started getting nervous, not being quite sure how to use that set up, but the next available bathroom for me turned out to be a regular toilet, so I guess they had a mix of both there. For the rest of the trip all the toilets were the sit down kind I'm used to.

We went through the museum, learning a bit about the difference between real lavender and lavendine, an easier to grow but less fragrant lavender look alike. Lavender oil is supposed to have healing, calming, soothing qualities. I bought some fine quality lavender oil for myself and a lavender candle and some lavender spray for two of my friends back home.

We didn't actually visit Gordes itself, but we stopped at a spot with a lovely view of the perched village to take some pictures. And then on to our first hotel, which was an old chateau, to unpack and have dinner.

## At the Chateau

An even row of tall shady trees lined either side of the narrow paved road leading to the Chateau. The old mansion sat at the end like a regal old woman with slightly shabby clothes and an unflappable disposition.

Rising three stories high, the weathered gray and white face was accented by faded mauve wooden shutters and doors. A worn balcony with balustrades sat halfway up the front of the building, jutting out precariously over an old stone courtyard below.

The entrance was around back. Just inside the giant wooden door was a box with hooks for the room keys, each designated by a wooden tag with a different color painted on it.

The old stone stairs at the back of the hall were so worn they seemed soft. The treads were narrow but not too steep, and the stuffed carcass of a dead wild animal loomed over the landing.

Wooden doors on either side of the stone corridors had large, wedge-shaped black hinges and giant keyholes for the old fashioned keys.

My roommate had requested a room with a view of the back garden, and we got the key for it and headed upstairs to unpack. The room was old and lovely. A bottle of wine waited for us on the table in the middle of the room and a heart shaped lavender soap was on each bed.

We each picked a bed, unpacked a bit, and got dressed for dinner. Then our group went to a little restaurant in the nearby village of Saint Remy. I sat next to one of the married men who was touring with his wife and he kept putting his arm across the back of my chair when he was relaxing, which was a bit too close for me. I wiggled around in the chair, moving it occasionally, hoping to dislodge his arm. But when he did remove it, it soon found its way back again. Dislike built up inside me, ostensibly for him but really for myself, since I was avoiding the confrontation of asking him if he could please keep his arm off the back of my chair. But it was a small thing, soon over, and when we headed back to the hotel I was relieved. But not for long.

My roommate and I settled down to go to sleep. As soon as she fell asleep she began snoring so loudly that I couldn't sleep. I tried putting my earplugs in but I could still hear it. Hour after hour went by. I got up again and again to  go to the bathroom and I grew more and more anxious as time passed. I may have dozed off for a bit after 1 or 2 AM only to wake before dawn. I waited quietly for it to get a bit light out, and then I left the room and went outside to explore around the grounds a bit and maybe sit quietly and rest.

I unlocked the giant back door lock and let myself out into the early morning air. I walked through the pebbled dining area, past the metal tables and chairs used for the outdoor breakfast to be served in another few hours.  I kept going and came to an old swimming pool with dark green water and enormous fish swimming in its depths. At the edge of the pool were three Roman busts, statues that stood guarding over the pool.

I went into the olive groves. The trees were lined up in even rows across the field, and in between masses of red poppies were growing. I had to walk on them sometimes to traverse the field.

One edge of the field had a stream running through it which probably fed the swimming pool I passed as well as the fountain back at the chateau.

I found a chair covered with dew and did my best to wipe it off and drag it over to a spot where some weak sun was breaking over the horizon, to try and keep warm while I waited. I decided that as soon as I saw Robbi again, I would ask if it was still possible to get a single room and pay the extra money. I was worried there wouldn't be any available and also worried about asking since I didn't want to be difficult (translated, I'm afraid of other people's opinions).

One of the other women on the tour who was traveling alone also came outside early and sat in a field sketching and writing in her notebook. Her name was Marlene, and she was a sweet, enthusiastic character filled with joie de vivre (the joy of life) as they say in France. She was the youngest person on the tour, only in her thirties.

I spent about three hours outside, alternating between enjoying the early morning sun and the lovely surroundings and anxiously wondering whether there would be any free rooms available once I explained my predicament to Robbi.

Finally, Robbi was up and about, getting people together for the day's adventure. I asked her if I could possibly get a single room and pay the extra costs, since I was having trouble sleeping with my roommate.

She was able to get me a room of my own at the chateau, but the next hotel didn't have an extra room available, so my roommate and I would be together again at the end of the week.

But I was overjoyed! At least I would have my own room for a few days and hopefully get the rest I needed to enjoy my trip. My roommate was as anxious to get separate quarters as I was, since apparently I woke her up every hour when I got up to use the toilet when I couldn't sleep – and I snored too! So happily, she agreed to split the extra cost.

My new room was across the hall from our old one and looked towards the front of the chateau. It was painted a soft yellow and had simple white curtains with blue and yellow flowers hung by brass rings over the two small windows sitting side by side, like a pair of kind eyes watching over the front drive.

I unlatched the glass pane windows and spread them open to enjoy the soft summer air. There were no screens for the windows and no need as only the very occasional fly lazily found its way into the room. I leaned out the window, feeling very secure since the walls were about a foot thick, peering down at an old bathtub with flowers planted inside sitting in the abandoned courtyard below.

Two girls who had wandered into the courtyard looked up at me. I called down, "Bonjour," and they answered in kind. Then they asked what the chateau was like inside.

"Formidable (great)," I replied.

"Is it worth staying in?" they inquired.

"Oui," was my simple but heartfelt response, as I had waited my whole life to be here.

## Feeling the Old Me

Once I got confirmation that I could have my own room for the next three days and I could move in right away, I relaxed. I told Robbi that I would stay behind that day and not go to the vineyard with the rest of the group. I moved into the yellow room right away, and laid down on the bed in complete gratitude. After a nap, catching up on some of my missed sleep, I decided to try taking a walk to the nearby village.

I walked along the little lane that led from the chateau to the main road leading into St. Remy de Provence (pronounced San rayMe de proVonce, with a little bit of a ruffle to the r's). It felt so good to be walking in the sun, having come a little way with a little way to go. I wasn't wearing myself out with a lot of talking, not being fluent in French. I was by myself actually on my brave adventure. I had a bottle of water in my bag, and I took sips from it as I became thirsty. It was quiet… no one else was on the road. A sign for a little house or perhaps an inn swung lazily in the breeze. I clopped along, my feet hurting a bit after my much longer than anticipated hike to Notre Dame de la Guard two days before. But I felt strong and I could take my time.

I felt the girl I used to be years and years before come up inside of me. I felt like I left her behind a long time ago in my misguided quest for love. But I could feel her, finally, as I relaxed into the walk. I traveled hundreds of miles from home, by myself, in a country where I barely speak the language, to let go of enough to find her buried in there, but still alive. I think she's connected straight to God without the interference of a lot of thinking. She never wonders whether life is worth living, because she knows it is. Her little dreams are of writing and traveling. She has no big dream of being married or having a husband. She dreams only of what she might do on her own and of freedom. She's not preoccupied with finding a boyfriend because she likes herself fine and enjoys the pleasure of her own company.

She was the tomboy who loved to wear jeans and run with the boys and play outside and ride her bike. She went on long walks and adventures to the dump and the big park in the next town over, getting lost on the way home. She didn't worry about what was going to happen. She enjoyed eating grapes off the vine and wild sour rhubarb and sucking the end of the little purple clovers to get at the sweet juice. She enjoyed the feeling of using her body to hike and run and play, pleasantly exhausted by physical activity at the end of the day. She was not afraid to learn a new language. She was not yet discouraged. I was glad to find her.

## Saint Remy

When I arrived in Saint Remy I oriented myself to the big church at the head of the square and then began to wander around. There was a big oval on the outside of town lined with shops and outdoor cafes. Winding lanes led inside the oval where there were more shops and some places to live too. Every time I went down one of the twisting interior lanes I got disoriented, but I could always find my way once I got to the outside of the oval.

I found a drugstore where I purchased some bandaids for the blisters developing on the bottom of my feet. They said "lavable" on the box, which I ignored as unimportant at the time of purchase. But it turned out it meant "cuttable." The bandaid was one long strip of bandaid, and I needed to cut off the amount I wanted to use. I had never seen anything like that back home and thought it was a great idea to create my own size, as required. But I didn't have any scissors, so I couldn't use it yet.

I looked inside clothing shops and found a tank top with material to create a little bow sewed onto one shoulder. It reminded me of the girls at the front desk in the hotel in Marseilles so I bought it. I browsed through the food store, getting a fresh bottle of water and a little snack. I got bread at the bakery and ate it for lunch sitting on a stoop. Then I headed back to the hotel where I met up with everyone for dinner.

The next morning, we went to market day. It was fabulous – colorful, vibrant, and filled with vendors selling all kinds of goods as well as food. They sold linens and dishtowels and woven baskets and clothes and food – everything!

I bought 3 apricots from a fruit vendor. I thought I would get to select my own from the top of the pile but he handed me 3 not so good ones instead. Lesson learned. I tossed the apricots in the trash and decided I needed to be more careful. I purchased a little pair of scissors, which I immediately used to cut my "lavable" bandaids to size while I sat on the curb. I put them over the blisters on the bottom of my feet. That felt much better.

Shopping at the market was everything wonderful I imagined it would be. I found a woman who sold pareos. I talked to her for a while and looked through what she had to sell. I bought four in the end, some for gifts.

The vendor showed me how to wrap the pareo a few different ways but I only remembered one. I practiced it a couple of times, so I wouldn't forget when I got home. She was very nice and taught me to say "Bon journee" instead of "Bonjour" when I was leaving people after being with them for a bit.

I walked through the vendor's booths lining both sides of the narrow streets looking at various food items, but only buying a lemon sorbet for a snack. At the top of the street across from the big church, the square was filled with more vendors. I bought a blue, green and cream colored skirt, two dishtowels, and a couple of music CDs. One was a popular French song and the other had a song from the movie "Chocolat." I also bought two silk scarves, and I was able to negotiate a slight discount for buying two instead of just one, which is something I'm never usually brave enough to do. It was a fun shopping experience.

## Avignon

We arrived at the bottom of the main street in Avignon early in the morning on Wednesday. One of the guys was a pretty good singer, and we strolled up the street singing Simon and Garfunkle's old tune "The Boxer" out loud, with the rest of our group in front of us or behind us. It was too early for the shops to be open but we could look in the display windows as we followed Robbi up the hill. We passed the carousel at the top of the street and went along further to the Palace of the Popes where apparently the Pope built a second home and stayed for a while when Italy was a bit too dangerous.

We cut through a narrow street and came to a lovely old hotel with a plant filled terrace bathed in early morning sun. Our gourmet cooking class was in the basement down some narrow, twisted stone steps. The kitchen was huge and beautiful, with a gigantic old wood stove at the head of the room. A long large table ran down the middle with stools on either side to accommodate all of us.

A famous Provencal chef who spoke only French was about to show us how to make a meal with the assistance of a younger bi-lingual chef who agreed to assist with the language barrier.

On the table was a giant grass green glass bowl filled with large, beautiful apricots, glowing orange with a ripe red blush. These would be part of our dessert.

There was fresh fish from the fish market – sardines and anchovies – which had to be gutted and filleted. Fortunately, as I was very busy writing down the details of the recipes I was spared the fish-gutting task. Later, they were delicious fried, with a light tomato sauce over them.

The main course was rabbit which I had never eaten before. But I decided since France was famous for fine food, I would at least try everything that was offered to me (other than the wine). Everything was delicious. I asked the chef in French if he ate like that all the time and he smiled and said, "No, this meal would be a Sunday dinner." I asked him if he wanted me to help him in the kitchen with the dessert, which was chocolate mousse with apricots. He showed me how to scoop the mousse out with a large spoon just so and arrange two scoops on a plate with the apricots.

After dessert, the chef left. As he was saying goodbye he looked right at me and blew me a kiss, I think because I spoke French with him. I was so happy! Although my French is not too good, my efforts were certainly being appreciated.

After cooking class and then eating the fruits of our labors, we had a few hours for shopping. I spent some of the time in a video store trying to find a current popular French movie that had English subtitles. Though the store clerk tried a couple in their machine none of the French possibilities had the English translations. I knew without them I would not understand enough of what was being said, so after an hour or so of working at the project, I came away empty handed.

Next, I hurried through the shopping district trying to assess what was available so I could make my best choices. In one store I explained I was hoping to find a blue sweater. The woman who waited on me went up in the storage area while I waited in the shop and found exactly what I had been hoping for – a muted blue V neck sweater. I bought a couple of T shirts at Petit Bateau, two yellow pottery mugs with a red flowers on them, and a last minute purchase of outrageously high shoes that I will surely almost never wear. I raced back to the meeting place to join the rest of our party who were already assembled and waiting to go to supper.

I wore a scarf to dinner just hanging straight down from either side of my neck. Various members of the tour took turns showing me their preferred method of how to wear it, to enlarge my fashion options. The truth is I'll only wear it the one way but it was fun to see them try.

During our tour that week, we went to a renowned restaurant where we had the most fantastic lunch imaginable. The main entrée was pigeon which is not something I would have ordered. But I ate it and it was good. And the dessert was some kind of amazing mousse with berries served in champagne type glasses with dry ice sending wisps of fog around as it was served.

We visited old Roman ruins and a place where Vincent van Gogh spent his last months painting, going crazy, and dying. We went to the most fantastic cave, that had classical music playing and showed giant pictures painted by the famous artist Monet, lit up on the walls in larger than life images. Outside it was hot, but the cave was cool. The pictures were projected onto many walls and kept changing to different pieces of the artist's work. As I walked through I was completely absorbed by the unbelievable art and classical music. Our tour guide Jim came up to me and asked me if I liked it, and I said it was just incredible. He said, "Take your time, come out when you're ready," but I knew that would be too long for him to wait.

My impressions of France were wonderful. Dogs drinking from fountains in town squares, hanging out in their owner's shops while they worked and going to outdoor restaurants with their people. There was outdoor dining almost everywhere with few mosquitoes to drive people indoors. Fresh bread, delicious chocolates, lots of walking. Peach or tan stucco houses with French blue shutters and red tile roofs. Something good inside me came out in that festive, informal environment where the language was music to my ears, even though it was mostly words I didn't understand. I didn't have to understand with my head to know I loved it with my heart.

At the end of the week, I was happy to be going home and delighted that I had come.

## The Red Sneaker

I am not a farm girl – I grew up in a suburb of Boston which had neighborhoods and sidewalks and buses that you could catch from in front of the bank downtown. When I was a little kid we had a milkman who came and delivered the milk, but at some point while I was growing up the milk truck stopped coming and we got our milk at the supermarket.

I like the feel of the country – it relaxes me to get out where there's less traffic and more trees, and windy roads without lots of people living on them. So I moved to a town far from the city, beyond the suburbs, in a more rural setting. The town had a working dairy farm which still delivered milk right to people's houses.

For a while my ex-boyfriend Dick worked on this dairy farm delivering milk. The farm had cows on the premises that were milked every day unlike some places that deliver milk they get from another farm somewhere else. One time he took me to see the farm. I wore my jeans and a sweatshirt, and on my feet my brand new low cut red Converse All Stars sneakers.

When we got to the farm we went through the little store that sold milk and a few other things. There were some dusty old milk bottles from many different farms, high up on the top shelf as a decoration. In the refrigerators there were old fashioned thick glass bottles of whole, low fat and skim milk, plus delicious dark chocolate milk made from their own secret recipe.

In the back of the store there was a door that led out to where the cows' stalls were. The stalls were lined up on either side of a broad walkway covered with hay and sawdust.

Dick told me to watch where I was walking and I said OK. Then I saw a baby cow in one of the stalls, and I walked over for a closer look.

When I stepped up close to the stall, my left foot sank down in about a foot of cold water, filling up my sneaker and soaking my socks and pant leg. It turns out there was a trough that ran next to the stalls on either side of the walkway, but the straw and sawdust floated on the top, making it blend right in with the concrete walkway until stepped on. The trough was filled with icy cold water mixed with cow shit and whatever else needed to be washed out of those stalls.

The cold, wet feeling of my lower leg and foot took a little bit of the thrill of being at the farm away, but I was relatively undaunted by the problem as I visited the cows. It wasn't until we got to the pigs and I got a chance to inhale their pungent aroma that I decided I'd had enough and wanted to go home.

Once I got home, I rinsed my sneaker out with the hose and set it on the back deck to dry. When it did, I realized it was a slightly darker color than my right sneaker, probably dyed a deeper hue from the cow manure potion that I stepped in. I was a little bummed out looking at that sneaker until I realized I am like the deep red sneaker.

I'm not too new anymore and I've been through some stuff that might make the color of my past seem a little dark. But I'm richer for it. I have gone through my stuff and come out triumphant on the other side. I've grown to appreciate my past for where it's gotten me today – a kinder, more compassionate, more spiritual person than I would have been if I stayed bright untarnished red.

I actually preferred the new color of my left sneaker, and I liked the reminder the contrast between the two gave me.

## Little Dreams

The thing about my big dream of being in a wonderful relationship is, even though I hung on the word of every romantic fairy tale, even though I asked people how they met and interviewed them about true love, whether it existed and how they recognized it, even though I memorized the romantic movies that resonated within me, the ones where people lived happily ever after, I don't think I ever really believed it. I had the heart of a cynic and the soul of a skeptic, and so I lived much of my life trying to make the best out of whatever was handy at the time.

Trying to make do with what was handy was something I could not pull off. The misery my life became motivated me to ask God to turn my life around more than once. I don't think I really knew much of love. Perhaps what I knew was obsession and desire.

I used to think I was very trusting but that wasn't it really. It was just that I didn't want to have to wait and notice whether someone was trustworthy so I just told all and gave all. And was disappointed when I was bitten by the human nature I didn't bother to observe.

I have often lost a piece of my heart and bruised my soul in pursuit of my big dream. Maybe the fairy tales can be true, maybe they just can't be pursued. Maybe the part of the stories I missed, the most relevant part, is the waiting. To wait until I know it's right instead of just taking a shot, hoping it will be but thinking probably not. Maybe I just didn't wait long enough. Maybe this time I will wait.

In the past fifteen years since I have believed in God I've wondered why my desire for a partner hasn't been fulfilled. But lately I've been wondering where that desire comes from. Is it from the part of God that's within me? Or is it something that comes from outside of me? Maybe somewhere along the line I put too much stock into this desire for a long term, committed relationship. Deep down I have the idea that I'll be happier if I find the right guy, and since I want to be happier, I desire it.

But maybe the truth is I have to pursue the other desires inside me, like writing or traveling to France. And when I fully throw myself into the things I want for myself, maybe I'll find out I don't need the relationship after all. Maybe just as happiness is the by-product of being kind to others, maybe the kind of relationship I want is just a by-product of living my life and not something I can aim straight for.

I have no doubt misinterpreted God's guidance for me many times, and probably misunderstood some spiritual lessons as well. In many ways I have been a lost soul. But I think when I followed my little dream to Provence, I connected again with the heart that still beats with the same little dreams I always had, still alive inside a darker red sneaker me.

www.ingramcontent.com/pod-product-compliance
Lightning Source LLC
Chambersburg PA
CBHW060809050426
42449CB00008B/1607